Allosaurus

and other Jurassic Meat-Eaters

by Daniel Cohen

Capstone Press

MINNEAPOLIS

Printed in the United States of America.

Capstone Press • 2440 Fernbrook Lane • Minneapolis, MN 55447

Editorial Director	John Coughlan
Managing Editor	Tom Streissguth
Production Editor	James Stapleton
Book Design	Timothy Halldin

Library of Congress Cataloging-in-Publication Data

Cohen, Daniel, 1936-
    Allosaurus and other Jurassic meat-eaters / Daniel Cohen.
        p. cm. -- (Dinosaurs of North America)
    Includes bibliographical references (pp. 38-39) and index.
    Summary: Describes four dinosaurs from the Jurassic
period including Allosaurus, Dilophosaurus, Ceratosaurus,
and Coelurus.
    ISBN 1-56065-286-1
    1. Allosaurus--Juvenile literature. 2. Dilophosaurus--
Juvenile literature. 3. Ceratosaurus--Juvenile literature. 4.
Coelurus--Juvenile literature. [1. Dinosaurus. 2.
Paleontology--Jurassic.] I. Title. II. Series: Cohen, Daniel,
1936- Dinosaurs of North America.
    QE862.S3C55 1996
    567.9'7--dc20   95-11243
                                                     CIP
                                                     AC

Table of Contents

Chapter 1

When They Lived

Millions of years ago, long before humans appeared, dinosaurs ruled the earth. It was an age of giants. The largest land creatures that ever lived walked on our planet. It was the **Jurassic** period.

The Jurassic period lasted from about 195 million to 140 million years ago. Think about that. Modern human beings have been on earth for only about 40,000 years. That gives you an idea of just how long the Jurassic (joo-RASS-ic) period lasted and how long ago it was.

Quaternary Age
1.8m to present

65m   Tertiary Age   1.8m

140m Cretaceous Age 65m   } Birds

195m Jurassic Age   140m   Mammals

230m Triassic Age   195m

280m Permian Age   230m   } Reptiles

345m Carboniferous 280m   Amphibians

395m Devonian Age 345m

435m Silurian Age   395m   } Fish

500m Ordovcian Age 435m   Primitive chordat

700m Cambrian Age 500m

Dinosaurs first appeared on the earth about 210 million years ago, during a period of geological time called the **Triassic** (try-ASS-ic) period. The earliest dinosaurs were fairly small and not very numerous. It was not until the Jurassic period that dinosaurs really became rulers of the land.

The Jurassic World

The Jurassic world was very different from our own. At one time all the land masses in the world were clumped together in a single supercontinent. By the Jurassic period the supercontinent had slowly begun to break up and drift apart. But the world's land masses were still a lot closer together than they are today.

The climate was very different as well. There were no polar ice caps and the range of temperatures worldwide was not nearly as great as it is now. The weather patterns were more regular and there were fewer severe storms.

Most Jurassic dinosaurs could probably have lived on land anywhere in the world.

Mammals and Plants

Dinosaurs were not the only creatures in the Jurassic world. They shared the land with small mammals, which resembled modern shrews and mice. Dinosaurs and our ancestors, the mammals, appeared on earth at about the same time. But for millions of years the dinosaurs were much more successful.

Jurassic plants were different than the plants we are familiar with today. There were no modern types of trees and no flowering plants. But ferns and cycads, which are primitive plants, grew nearly everywhere in the warm and swampy landscape. Some of these plants grew to enormous sizes and provided food for the large number of Jurassic **herbivorous**, or plant-eating, dinosaurs.

The Jurassic period lasted about 55 million years. During those millions of years the earth

changed. The continents drifted farther apart. The climate became less regular and uniform.

And during those millions of years the dinosaurs themselves changed. Dinosaurs that had flourished at the start of the Jurassic period became extinct by the end of the period. Many, many new species of dinosaurs first appeared during the Jurassic period. By the end of the period dinosaurs were far more successful and dominant than they had been at the beginning.

Allosaurus

(AL-oh-SAW-rus)
strange reptile
Range: *Western United States*
Length: *39 feet (11.7 meters)*
Weight: *2 tons (1.8 metric tons)*

Allosaurus was the largest and most fearsome **predator** of the Jurassic period. It had a large head and jaws filled with many

long, curved, and serrated teeth. Its neck was very heavy and strong. Its body was rather squat and supported by massive pillarlike hind legs.

Its tail was also massive and must have been very powerful. The tail would have provided balance when the creature ran on two legs. The front legs were small compared to the hind legs. Even so, they were powerful and ended in three viciously curved claws. A full-grown Allosaurus would have stood about 15 feet (4.5 meters) tall.

Allosaurus was a well equipped predatory dinosaur. The huge jaws lined with stabbing and cutting teeth could have been used both for killing and dismembering prey. The powerful neck and back would have aided the jaws in tearing off large chunks of flesh from its victims. The large claws on both front and back legs helped subdue victims.

Allosaurus bones have been found in Colorado and in other western states.

13

Although Allosaurus appears to have been built like a giant killing machine, some **paleontologists**–scientists who study ancient life–have wondered whether it really was an active predator at all. They think that it may have been too heavy and lumbering for active pursuit. These scientists think that Allosaurus was probably more of a **scavenger** that fed on the remains of already dead animals.

The majority opinion is that this creature pursued plant-eating dinosaurs like Stegosaurus and Diplodocus that were even heavier than themselves. Allosaurus did not have to move quickly, because its prey did not move quickly. Still, a single Allosaurus could not bring down prey that was three or four times larger than it was.

The plant-eating dinosaurs were not without their own defenses. Stegosaurus had a dangerous spiked tail and Diplodocus had an enormous tail that it could crack like a whip. Scientists believe that Allosaurus probably hunted in packs–a terrifying thought even millions of years later.

It seems possible that several Allosauruses might have been able to bring down a large dinosaur in a determined attack. It is probable that the main victims were less powerful juveniles. The plant-eaters probably gathered in herds to protect themselves from such attacks.

The fearsome Allosaurus had many long, curved teeth.

Like most predators Allosaurus was probably an opportunist. It hunted when it could find prey. It was a scavenger when it found an abandoned carcass. It drove smaller and weaker predators from their kills. In short, it ate whatever was available.

The bones of Apatosaurus, an enormous Jurassic plant-eater, have been found in the western United States with teeth marks on them similar to those of Allosaurus. Broken Allosaurus teeth have also been found scattered around the remains of other specimens of this plant-eater.

Allosaurus, which became extinct at the end of the Jurassic period, is the best known of the meat-eaters. The first remains of this dinosaur were uncovered in Colorado in the 1870s. Since then a large number of full and partial skeletons have been found. They represent the dinosaur at all stages of growth, from juvenile to adult. There must have been a large number of these fierce and gigantic predators during Jurassic times in order to leave so many remains behind.

Dilophosaurus

(Die-LOF-foh-SAW-rus)
two-crested reptile
Range: *Western United States*
Length: *20 feet (6 meters)*
Weight: *1 ton (.9 metric ton)*

The Dilophosaurus is the earliest known large Jurassic meat-eater that has been found. Its name comes from the two bony crests that run along the top of its skull. (In Greek, di means two and lophos means crest.)

The crests were too fragile to be used for protection. They may have been used for display during mating. Only the male Dilophosaurus appears to have had the crests.

Dilophosaurus flourished during the early Jurassic period. Experts believe it was the

Early Herbivore

Among the earliest plant-eating dinosaurs,
Heterodontosaurus was about the size of a turkey. Like
many mammals, it had three kinds of teeth: small,
sharp incisors, canine-like tusks, and grinding teeth for
chewing plants.

Heterodontosaurus
South Africa

The Origin of Dinosaurs

Dinosaurs probably originated from a thecodont
ancestor. The first thecodonts were lowslung and
crocodile-like, but some eventually evolved into agile
...these efficient predators

Dilophosaurus's teeth were probably used for plucking and tearing at the flesh of its victims.

largest predator of its time and probably stood 10 feet (3 meters) tall. Although it was closely related to Allosaurus, it was not nearly as strongly or heavily built.

The Dilophosaurus Skull

The skull of Dilophosaurus is large in proportion to its body. The lower jaw is strong and full of long, sharp, thin teeth. The upper jaw has a cluster of teeth at the front separate from the others. The teeth were probably used for plucking and tearing at the flesh of victims rather than for biting.

While Dilophosaurus had a large head and strong jaws, it probably did not kill its victims by biting. The thin teeth and delicate head crest would have broken too easily in a head-on fight with a larger foe. It is more likely that the creature attacked and ripped its prey with its clawed legs. It could also have been a scavenger that fed on the remains of animals killed by stronger predators.

Armed to Hunt

It is probable that Dilophosaurus, like most meat-eating dinosaurs, was an opportunist. It would eat whatever was available. Its neck was long and flexible and controlled by powerful

muscles. Its tail was long and provided balance for the animal as it walked and ran on its long and powerful hind legs. The front limbs were short but strong. Its hand had four fingers, three of which had strong, sharp claws. The first finger was shorter and more powerful than the others.

Dilophosaurus **fossils** were first discovered in 1942 in northern Arizona. A team from the University of California was led to the site by Jesse Williams, a Navajo. They discovered the remains of three individual dinosaurs. One skeleton was almost complete and two were in fragments. The remains were not recognized as belonging to a new species until 1954. It was not given the name Dilophosaurus until 1970.

Paleontology, the scientific study of life in past ages, often moves slowly. Many years can pass from the time that a new fossil discovery is made until it is studied, described, and named. It can be even longer before the general public learns of the discovery.

Ceratosaurus

(SER-a-toe-SAW-rus)
horned reptile
Range: *Western United States*
Length: *20 feet (6 meters)*
Weight: *1 ton (.9 metric ton)*

The most striking feature of Ceratosaurus is the horn or large bony bump on its snout. This is the feature that gives the creature its name. (In Greek, kerat means horned.) Its function is not known. It may have been used by males during ritual head-butting battles for mates.

Ceratosaurus was an active predator. It had massive jaws, armed with sharp, curved teeth. Its short arms had four powerful, clawed fingers on each hand. The long hind legs had three clawed toes on each foot.

An unusual feature of this dinosaur was a narrow row of bony plates running down the center of the back and tail. These gave the animal the appearance of having a serrated crest. The purpose of these bony plates is unknown. They may have served as protection. They might also have been used as part of a temperature control system.

A number of different dinosaur species had crests and plates of various sizes on their backs. The most well known of these is the Jurassic period plant-eater, Stegosaurus. The possibility that this feature, which appears on so many different dinosaurs, was used to gain or lose heat has often been discussed by scientists.

There has been a lot of speculation on the way of life and hunting habits of Ceratosaurus.

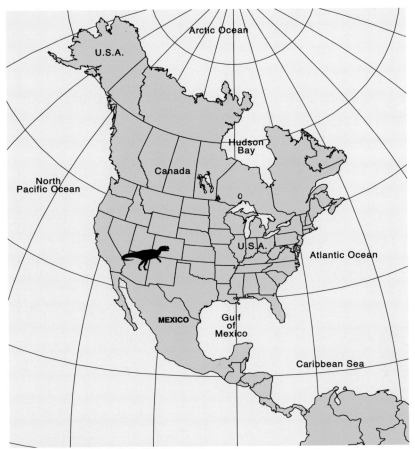

**Ceratosaurus remains are rare, perhaps because
this species was smaller than most other dinosaurs.**

It was clearly related to Allosaurus. But it
would seem to have been a smaller, lighter, and
more agile predator. While Allosaurus remains
are fairly common in Jurassic rocks, the
remains of Ceratosaurus, which lived at the

same time and in many of the same places, are quite rare. This might indicate that Ceratosaurus was a solitary predator. Allosaurus is believed to have been a pack hunter.

On the other hand, dinosaur footprints may present a very different picture of the life of the Ceratosaurus. In the western United States there are fossil-rich rocks called the Morrison Formation. Embedded in the formation's rocks are ancient dinosaur tracks, including footprints believed to be those of Ceratosaurus. Sometimes there is just a single footprint. In other places there are long trails of a dinosaur or group of dinosaurs, all made at the same time. These ancient trackways suggest that Ceratosauruses moved in groups and possibly hunted in packs to bring down larger dinosaurs.

There is a great deal about this rare and interesting Jurassic-era meat-eater that is not known. As with other dinosaurs, future discoveries may change our view of the way they lived nearly 200 million years ago.

Coelurus

(See-LOO-rus)
Hollow bones
Range: *Western United States*
Length: *7 feet (2.1 meters)*
Weight: *80 pounds (36 kilograms)*

Not all dinosaurs were lumbering giants. Many dinosaurs were small, light, and built for speed. One North American example was

Coelurus, whose name means hollow bones. The creature had hollow bones in its tail, which made it light for its size. Modern birds also have hollow bones.

Coelurus had a small head for its size. The skull would probably fit in the palm of your hand. Its legs were long and thin but well supplied with muscles. The tail would have provided balance while running. Its hands had three long, clawed fingers.

This dinosaur was built to be an active predator. It must have run through the swamps and forests of Jurassic North America catching prey with its claws. It would have fed on lizards, small flying reptiles, large insects, mammals, and even other small or immature dinosaurs. It probably ate anything it could catch and kill.

Smaller dinosaurs are not nearly as well known as many of their giant contemporaries. The small, light bones of these creatures would be less likely to be preserved and survive for tens of millions of years than the massive

bones of the giants. Small bones are also harder
to find and easier to overlook.

Small dinosaurs may have been far more
numerous and successful than the relatively
limited number of fossils indicate. Our

**The remains of Coelurus have been found in the
western United States.**

knowledge of life in Jurassic times is based in large part on accidental discoveries. We simply know more about those creatures that left behind well-preserved fossils than we do about the others.

Coelurus and its close relatives must have resembled such modern flightless birds as the secretary bird and the road runner. These birds run swiftly along the ground catching lizards, snakes, and other small prey.

The resemblance to small birds may be more than coincidental. Many scientists now believe that some of the close relatives of Coelurus eventually evolved into birds. If that is true, dinosaurs are not completely extinct. It would mean that the sparrows or robins hopping around in your back yard right now have dinosaurs somewhere in their background.

Chapter 3

How Dinosaurs are Discovered

We know that dinosaurs roamed the earth millions of years ago. Yet their remains continue to be discovered by scientists even now. How is it possible that dinosaur bones can be preserved for so many years? The answer lies in the process of fossilization.

When a dinosaur died, several different things could happen to its body. Animals may have eaten its flesh. Smaller animals and even bacteria could have eaten and removed the soft tissue of the dinosaur. Many times, the

A paleontologist carefully digs for remains of a dinosaur skeleton.

dinosaur bones could have been crushed or broken as the flesh was removed from the skeleton. So it is possible that many dinosaur bones simply disintegrated before they could be preserved by nature.

Turning into Rock

However, many dinosaur remains in desert climates were covered with windblown sand before they could be eaten or decompose. Others were washed into lakes or rivers and covered with mud. As the years went by, more and more sand and mud covered these dinosaurs. Over time, this sand and mud turned into rock. Over the course of thousands of years, chemicals in the rocks seeped into the dinosaur remains and turned them into rock, too. The hardened dinosaur remains are then called fossils.

Footprints made by dinosaurs have also been preserved by becoming fossils. So have dinosaur eggs, nests, and dung. All dinosaur fossils provide scientists with valuable information about these incredible animals and their life on earth.

Buried in Rock

Dinosaur fossils have been found on every continent on earth. In most cases, they are buried in rock. Scientists attempt to unearth the

fossils carefully with as little damage as possible to the remains.

The first step in excavating, or removing the fossils from the earth, is to take away the surrounding soil and rock. Large diggers and bulldozers do this work until the fossils are close to the surface. Then scientists work with small hand tools like hammers and chisels to remove the remaining rock.

The fossilized bones of this Allosaurus were rebuilt into a complete skeleton.

Careful Record-Keeping

Once the fossils are exposed, the scientists take great care to record everything they find. Bones are measured and photographed. Extensive notes and diagrams record exactly how the skeleton parts are connected.

As the bones are removed from the digging site, they are numbered and recorded. Then they are carefully packed into padded crates. If a bone is weak or crumbly, it is not removed until it is sprayed with a special hard-setting foam. Sometimes, plaster-soaked bandages are used to harden the bone.

Once all the fossils have been recorded from a site, they are carefully shipped to the scientists' laboratories. There the bones are rebuilt to show how the dinosaur looked while it was living and the dinosaurs ruled the earth.

Glossary

carnivorous–describes a species that can eat and digest meat

Cretaceous period–the third geological period in the Age of Dinosaurs, from 140 million to 65 million years ago

extinction–the death of a group of plants or animals

fossil–the remains of something that once lived

herbivorous–describes a species that lives on plants and vegetation

Jurassic period–the second geological period in the Age of Dinosaurs, from 195 million to 140 million years ago

paleontologists–scientists who study life in past ages

predator–an animal that hunts or preys upon other animals

scavenger–an animal that feeds upon dead or decayed matter

Triassic period–The first geological period in the Age of Dinosaurs, from 230 million to 195 million years ago

To Learn More

Aliki. *Dinosaurs Are Different.* New York: Crowell, 1985.

Arnold, Caroline. *Dinosaur Mountain: Graveyard of the Past.* New York: Clarion Books, 1989.

Benton, Michael. *The Dinosaur Encyclopedia.* New York: Julian Messner, 1984.

Cohen, Daniel and Cohen, Susan. *Where to Find Dinosaurs Today.* New York: Cobblehill, 1992.

Funston, Sylvia. *The Dinosaur Question and Answer Book* from *Owl* magazine and the Dinosaur Project. Boston: Little, Brown, 1992.

Lasky, Kathryn. *Dinosaur Dig.* New York: Morrow Junior Books, 1990.

Lauber, Patricia. *Dinosaurs Walked Here and Other Stories Fossils Tell*. New York: Bradbury Press, 1991.

Lindsay, William. *The Great Dinosaur Atlas*. New York: Julian Messner, 1991.

Most, Bernard. *Where to Look for a Dinosaur*. Orlando, Fla.: Harcourt Brace Jovanovich, 1993.

Murphy, Jim. *The Last Dinosaur*. New York: Scholastic, 1988.

Sattler, Helen R. *The Solar-Powered Dinosaurs*. New York: Lothrop, Lee & Shepard Books, 1992.

Stefoff, Rebecca. *Extinction*. New York: Chelsea House Publishers, 1992.

Wallace, Joseph E. *The Audubon Society Pocket Guide to Dinosaurs*. New York: Knopf, 1993.

Some Useful Addresses

The Academy of Natural Sciences
19th Street and The Parkway
Philadelphia, PA 19103

The American Museum of Natural History
Central Park West at 79th Street
New York, NY 10024-5192

California Academy of Sciences
Golden Gate Park
San Francisco, CA 94118-4599

Dinosaur National Monument
P.O. Box 210
Dinosaur, CO 81610

Field Museum of Natural History
Roosevelt Road at Lake Shore Drive
Chicago, IL 60605-2496

Museum of the Rockies
South Sixth Street and Kagy Boulevard
Bozeman, MT 59717-0040

National Museum of Natural History
Smithsonian Institution
Tenth Street and Constitution Avenue N.W.
Washington, DC 20002

**Natural History Museum of Los Angeles
 County**
900 Exposition Boulevard
Los Angeles, CA 90007

New Mexico Museum of Natural History
1801 Mountain Road
Albuquerque, NM 87104

The Peabody Museum
170 Whitney Avenue
New Haven, CT 06511

Royal Ontario Museum
100 Queen's Park
Toronto, Ontario M5S 2C6
Canada

Tyrell Museum of Paleontology
Box 7500
Drumheller, Alberta T0J 0Y0
Canada

Where to View Tracks

Dinosaur Ridge

This is a national landmark near Morrison, west of Denver, Colorado. The hiking trail allows visitors to stroll along a trackbed from the Cretaceous period.

Dinosaur Valley State Park

This park is in Glen Rose, southwest of Fort Worth, Texas. Part of an original dinosaur trackway was excavated here. It is on view at the American Museum of Natural History in New York City.

Dinosaur State Park

Visitors to this park, in Rocky Hill, south of Hartford, Connecticut, can make plaster casts of dinosaur tracks.

For more information on dinosaur events and sites, write to:

Dinosaur Society
200 Carleton Avenue
East Islip, NY 11730
(516) 277-7855

This organization promotes research and education in the study of dinosaurs. It also publishes *Dino Times*, a monthly magazine for children. Subscriptions are $19.95 a year. *Dinosaur Report*, a quarterly magazine, costs $25 a year.

Index

Photo credits: Cheryl R. Richter: pp. 4, 10-11, 34; Linda J. Moore: pp. 18-19; Bruce Selyem, Museum of the Rockies: p. 32

47